ANN STIRLAND

HUMAN BONES
IN ARCHAEOLOGY

SHIRE ARCHAEOLOGY

Cover photograph
Skeletons of a pregnant woman and her foetus
from the Monastery Museum of Aebelholt, Denmark.
(Photograph: National Museum, Copenhagen.)

British Library Cataloguing in Publication Data available

Published by
SHIRE PUBLICATIONS LTD
Cromwell House, Church Street, Princes Risborough,
Aylesbury, Bucks HP17 9AJ, UK

Series Editor: James Dyer

ISBN 0 85263 759 4

First published 1986

Set in 11 point Times and printed in Great Britain by
C. I. Thomas & Sons (Haverfordwest) Ltd,
Press Buildings, Merlins Bridge, Haverfordwest, Dyfed.

Contents

4

List of illustrations

Preface

In the past many archaeologists disliked being faced with human skeletal remains when excavating a site. Such remains are difficult to excavate and their presence serves to emphasise our common mortality. Until recent, more enlightened times they were often ignored or thrown away. It is now appreciated that the excavation and study of these remains is of great interest and importance to archaeology. There are three main reasons why this work is of such importance.

Firstly, the study of a particular burial group provides accurate evidence of the physical characteristics of a previous community, either archaeological or historical. Anthropometric data, such as the calculation of stature based on the measurement of long bones, may be obtained, together with information on the physical well-being or otherwise of a group. Patterns of diet and nutrition may be studied, together with diseases, accidents and customs, all of which leave their marks on the bones.

Secondly, groups of skeletons are the major source of evidence for the pattern of ancient diseases and of their subsequent evolution.

Lastly, fossilised bones from places such as Olduvai Gorge present the only evidence for the fossil forms of the human race and of the patterns of its evolution.

This book is an introduction to the study of skeletal remains for the non-specialist who has an interest in all aspects of archaeology.

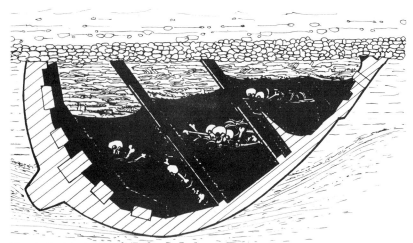

Fig. 1. Burials in the *Mary Rose*. Burial in anaerobic silts has produced this kind of preservation. See also plate 1.

Plate 1. Well preserved bones from the *Mary Rose*.

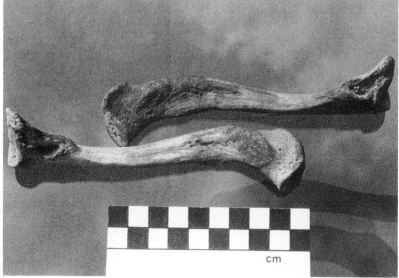

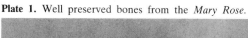

1
Burial conditions and preservation; the dating and treatment of bones

Like other organic remains, the preservation of human burials depends largely on the conditions of their burial and the nature of the deposits in which they have been placed. Where burial is deliberate, as is usually the case, the accompanying rituals may also affect preservation.

Bone is composed of both mineral and organic materials, in the ratio of approximately two to one. The chief mineral is calcium, mainly as phosphate, while the main organic material is the protein collagen. The process of removal of the minerals is called decalcification and occurs when bone is soaked for some time in dilute mineral acids, leaving the organic components untouched. Such waterlogged acidic conditions occur in some lakes and in peat bogs, resulting in the preservation of complete bodies in some cases. The most famous examples of this kind of burial are the preserved bodies of the Tollund and Grauballe men, dating from the iron age in Denmark (Glob, 1973), and the preserved adult male body from Lindow Moss in Cheshire.

In waterlogged anaerobic conditions, where oxygen is excluded and bodies are buried in silt, preservation of the bones will be good, providing the silts are alkaline. The absence of oxygen means that the bacteria which break down organic remains cannot survive. The burials from the Tudor warship the *Mary Rose* have been preserved in this way and the bones are very hard and well preserved (fig. 1 and plate 1).

Quick burial, often as a result of natural disaster, will preserve bone and allow fossilisation to occur, should the surrounding matrix be rich in mineral salts of iron and calcium. The organic components are gradually replaced by these salts, while the form of the bone is retained. This appears to have occurred with some of the *Mary Rose* burials (Rule, 1982). In cases where the natural disaster has been in the form of a volcanic eruption covering everything with dust, whole skeletons may be preserved, as at Herculaneum.

Graves occurring in a well aerated, damp, acid soil such as porous sand are almost always empty, since both the organic and the mineral parts of bone are attacked under these acidic conditions (fig. 2). Alternatively, in areas of extreme aridity such

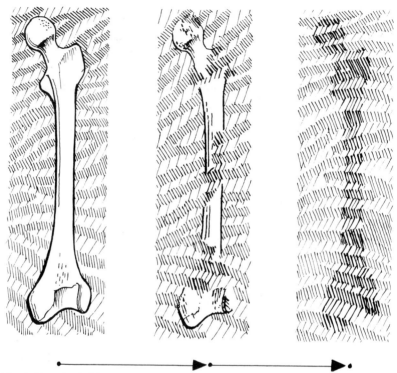

Fig. 2. Bone buried in acidic soil. Burial in acidic soil such as sand destroys bone very efficiently.

as around the Dead Sea, entire bodies may be preserved by natural dehydration in the desert sands. Thus at Masada whole plaits of human hair were preserved, in Egypt Predynastic corpses have survived and in the south-western states of North America there are many natural native American 'mummies'. Burials in wooden coffins in alkaline soils, such as bronze age barrows in Denmark, are sometimes reasonably well preserved.

While these examples are extreme, most burial conditions have some features of the soil types discussed, and in some graves and burial grounds conditions may be mixed, so that preservation of bones will vary both within and between graves.

The two rituals which most affect the preservation of bone are mummification and cremation. Mummification may be deliberate as in the Pharaonic burials of ancient Egypt, or by accidental

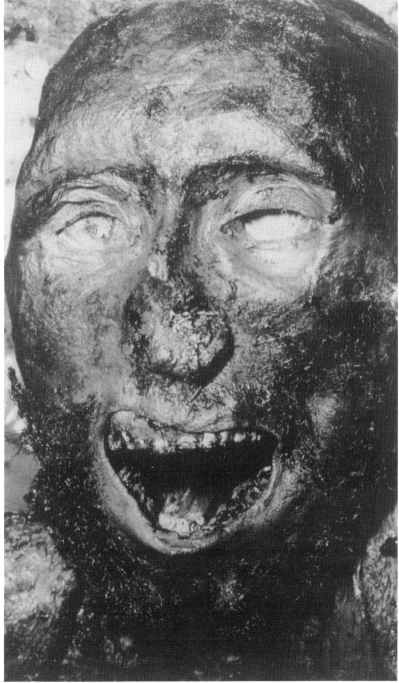

Plate 2. The St Bee's mummy. One of the few surviving examples of mummification in Europe, in this case deliberate. (Photograph: P. Kershaw.)

dehydration as shown above. Mummification may have been practiced in Great Britain, although the evidence has not survived subsequent burial conditions except for the St Bee's mummy from Egremont, Cumbria, found in 1981 (plate 2).

Cremation destroys the organic content of bone when it is exposed to relatively low red heat for a long time. The bone left retains its shape but is dead white in colour, light and fragile. This process is known as calcination. With prehistoric cremations bodies were often burnt only long enough to reduce them to bones which could then be broken into uniform fragments for insertion into a container such as an urn for burial. The cremation techniques were often inefficient, leaving poorly burnt bones which retain plenty of evidence for the anthropologist (Clay, 1981).

Dating

Material may be dated archaeologically either relatively or absolutely. Relative dating depends on the accurate assignment to a specific time of the artefact which may be found in the same context as a particular skeleton. These artefacts may consist of personal ornaments or possessions which belonged to the dead person, or items associated with daily life. Older, sometimes extinct forms such as palaeolithic hunters or Neanderthals may be dated in this manner by examination of any associated stone tools, animal bones or fossil plant materials, as well as by the actual stratified deposits in which the skeleton or bones may lie. In cases where associated objects or the burial are intrusive, that is cutting into and through various deposits, these methods of relative dating are inapplicable, since the burial is obviously later than the deposits (fig. 3).

Absolute dating methods are used far less with archaeological material, particularly human bone, since they are either unsuitable or destructive in operation and always expensive. The best known is *radiocarbon dating*. This is dating by measurement of the amount of radioactive carbon -14 still present in dead organic remains.

Atmospheric nitrogen-14 becomes carbon-14 as a result of cosmic ray bombardment. This known amount of carbon-14 is incorporated in atmospheric carbon dioxide, which in turn is absorbed first by plant and then by animal tissues. When the animal dies the absorption of carbon-14 ceases, and its proportion within the dead organism decreases at a constant rate, as it converts back to nitrogen-14 again. This steady decrease (half-

Fig. 3. An intrusive burial. This grave has been cut through various stratified levels, making the dating of the burial very difficult.

recent
tree

ancient
tree

TS.

life) of carbon is 5730 years, or the length of time it takes for about half the original amount of carbon-14 in the sample to be converted. The decay is constant and the results are accurate to about plus or minus 5 per cent. This method is particularly useful for dating archaeological materials, since carbon-14 has a relatively short half-life and therefore can be used for dating organic materials up to seventy thousand years old. The method has been found to produce errors in the dating of more recent materials and these errors have been corrected by the application of dendrochronology.

Dendrochronology is the counting and correlation of the tree-ring patterns found on the cut surfaces of recent and of ancient trees, and of wooden artefacts (fig. 4). Since it depends on the accurate matching of these patterns back to the living tree, it can be used only within the lifespan of the oldest living suitable tree (the Californian bristlecone pine), which is about the last five thousand years. However, it has been found to be particularly accurate when dating wooden artefacts from the last one thousand years. For this period dendrochronology was shown to be more accurate than carbon-14 and is therefore used to correct these more recent radiocarbon dates. Dendrochronology could be used to date a well preserved coffin, and therefore the burial within it.

Other methods of dating may be used archaeologically, but they do not apply to human bones.

The treatment of bones

Human bones should be treated with care and respect both on and off the site and certain simple rules should be followed to facilitate both preservation and study.

Every bone or fragment should be saved. No fragment is too insignificant for the anthropologist to study.

The bones should be left in place until the whole skeleton has been exposed.

The skeleton should be photographed, with a suitable scale, before removal.

Every effort should be made to remove the skeleton on the day it is exposed in case the bones are disturbed or stolen.

Fig. 4. Dendrochronology. Dating of wooden artefacts by the comparison of the tree-ring patterns on their cut surfaces and those of trees back into antiquity.

Very accurate records of the surviving bones should be taken before any bones are removed.

A skeleton should be excavated with great care and placed in correctly marked containers such as paper bags.

After excavation, bone should be cleaned and each piece carefully marked. Cleaning should take place over a screen, so that small fragments such as teeth do not disappear down the sink. If necessary, a soft brush should be used to clean the bones. The marking ink should be waterproof, and the marks very clear and visible.

Never work on two skeletons at the same time. Natural mixing is bad enough to cope with.

Never pick up a skull by the eye sockets; always handle bones with great care and skulls with both hands.

2
The identification of bones

Unfortunately, on an archaeological site human burials do not always come in convenient grave packages. Often disturbances of some kind have occurred, causing mixing of the human bones. This kind of mixing reaches extreme proportions in the case of a ship burial, such as the *Mary Rose*. In other circumstances human and animal remains become mixed. On some sites, particularly prehistoric ones, animal bones may have been deliberately buried in a barrow or tomb as part of the ritual. On others, the mixing may be accidental, where, for example, a site has been used over a very long period and a burial ground has been subsequently re-used for midden heaps or rubbish pits. The later cutting of a well or pit not only mixes interred human bones but often contains animal bones within the rubbish.

Although animal and human skeletons are quite different there are similarities between individual bones of some species that can make differentiation on site difficult. An excellent and extremely useful text for dealing with this problem is *Bones for the Archaeologist* by Dr I. W. Cornwall. Generally differences in size (fish and bird bone) and in means of locomotion (animals are quadruped) indicate bones that are not human.

The human skeleton

It will be useful at this stage to introduce some fundamental terms that should be understood. When discussing these, it is assumed that the individual is standing erect with arms at the sides and palms of the hands facing to the front. In this position all the bones of the skeleton are lying straight and uncrossed in relation to each other (see fig. 5). This is known as the *correct anatomical position*.

The following terms are used to describe relative positions of structures in all skeletons.

Median sagittal plane (MSP): the central plane of the body which passes along the central sagittal suture in the top of the skull, and about which the body is bilaterally symmetrical and divided into right and left halves.
Frontal section: divides the body into front and rear portions.
Lateral: any structure which lies furthest away on a bone, or on the skeleton, to the MSP.

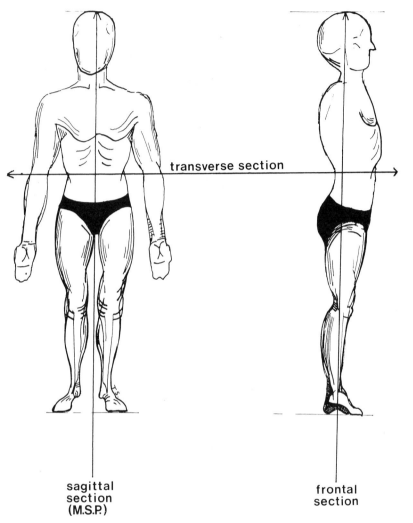

Fig. 5. Correct anatomical position.

Medial: any structure which is relatively nearer on a bone, or on a skeleton, to the MSP.

Transverse: any feature which is at right angles to the MSP.

Anterior (ventral), posterior (dorsal), superior, inferior: terms used to denote front, back, up and down when describing the skeleton or individual bones.

Proximal; distal: relatively close to and away from the vertebral column or head. These terms are used when describing the limbs. Hands and feet are known as the *extremities.*

Special terms are used when describing teeth, although these terms are still used in relation to the MSP (fig. 6).

Mesial: the surface of a tooth which is towards the middle of the mouth or the MSP.

Distal: the surface of a tooth which faces away from the MSP.

Lingual: the surface of a tooth which faces the tongue.

Buccal: the surface of a premolar or molar tooth which faces the cheek.

Labial: the surface of an anterior tooth which faces the lips.

Occlusal: the chewing surface of all teeth.

When a body has been buried face downwards, this position is known as *prone.* When it is lying on its back, it is *supine.* When the fore or lower arm is held at a right angle to the upper arm and the palm of the hand is held down towards the ground, this position is known as *pronation;* when the palm is held upwards, the position is *supination.*

A joint is said to be *flexed* when held at an angle, and *extended* when held in a straight line. When the arms are spread and the legs straddled the limbs are said to be *abducted;* when the arms are at the sides and the legs together they are *adducted.*

The *axial skeleton* consists of the skull, vertebral column, sternum and ribs, and the *appendicular skeleton* consists of the limbs. Where bones come together, as in joints, they *articulate.* *Cartilage* is the tissue which covers such articular surfaces, and the skeleton therefore consists of the solid bony framework and of cartilage.

A step-by-step guide to the human skeleton.
There are usually 206 bones in the adult skeleton (fig. 7),
falling into four groups.

1. Long bones
These are all paired bones, there being six pairs, three in each
limb. They perform all the large movements and partly support

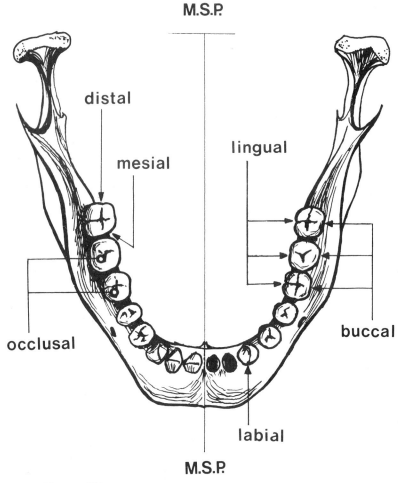

Fig. 6. The mandible.

skull

cervical vertebrae

clavicle
scapula
manubrium
sternum
ribs
humerus

thoracic vertebrae

lumbar vertebrae

pelvis

sacrum
radius
ulna

carpals
metacarpals
phalanges

femur

patella

fibula

tibia

tarsals
metatarsals
phalanges

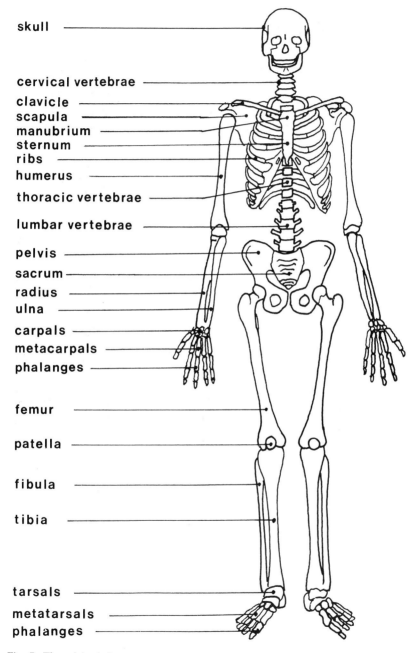

Fig. 7. The adult skeleton.

the body's weight: *arms* (humerus, radius and ulna); *legs* (femur, tibia and fibula). They all have tubular shafts and articular surfaces at each end. They are the largest, longest bones in the body.

Fig. 8. Right hand.

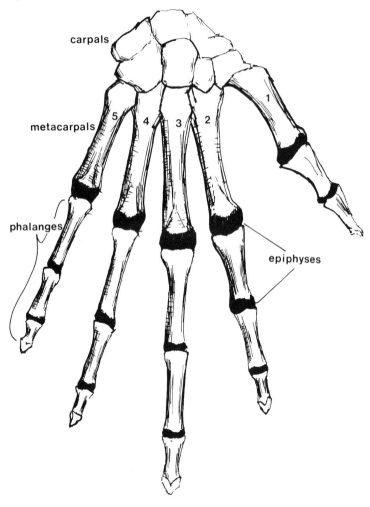

Fig. 9. Right foot.

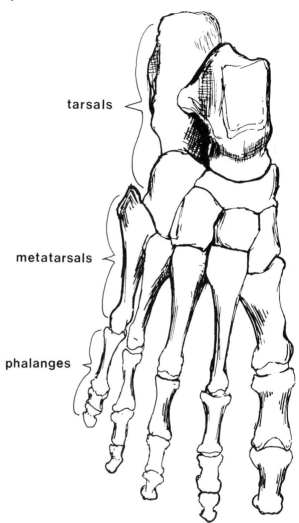

2. Short bones
 These are like the long bones in miniature, having both a similar structure and occurring in pairs from left to right: *hands* (five metacarpals and fourteen phalanges in each, fig. 8); *feet* (five metatarsals and fourteen phalanges in each, fig. 9); two *clavicles*, one on each side. They are used in all movements where flexibility, dexterity or precision is required.

3. Flat bones

These occur in areas where both protection and large supporting surfaces for the attachment of muscles are required: *skull* (the large, flat bones enclosing the brain); *pelvis* (two hip bones); *scapula* (two shoulder blades, one on each side, fig. 10); *ribs* (twenty-four, twelve on each side); *breastbone* (one manubrium, one sternum).

Fig. 10. Left scapula.

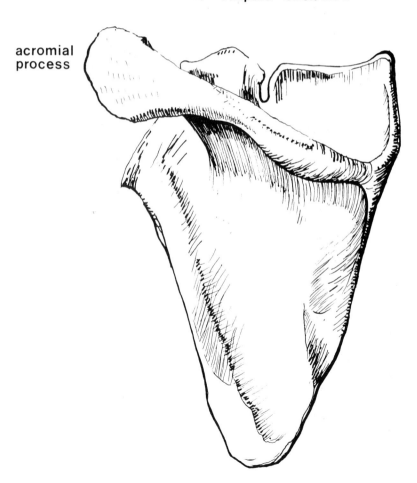

left scapula – back view

acromial
process

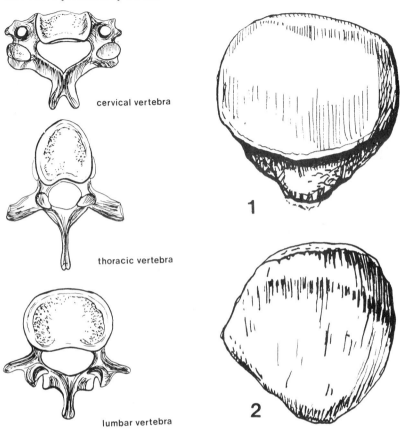

cervical vertebra

thoracic vertebra

lumbar vertebra

Fig. 11. *(Left).* Vertebrae.

Fig. 12. *(Right).* Left patella. 1, back; 2, front.

4. Irregular bones

These are often complex and odd in shape and have specialised functions: *vertebral column,* consisting of seven cervical, twelve thoracic, five lumbar and six sacral vertebrae (there may be some variation in these numbers and there may be more or less in the column) (fig. 11); *wrist* (eight carpal bones, fig. 8); *ankle* (seven tarsal bones, fig. 9); *kneecap* (two patellae, fig. 12).

3
Recording, measurement and primary data

The analysis of an individual skeleton must begin with the careful recording of every surviving bone or fragment. In the case of mixed burials, individuals must first be resorted by the matching of paired bones wherever possible and the use of criteria such as aging to put back together all those bones which belong to the same individual. This is a difficult and very subjective task, and its success partly depends on the condition of the surviving bone. In the case of the *Mary Rose*, for example, the condition of the bones is so superb that an attempt has been made to put skeletons back together for analysis.

Some archaeologists employ a skeleton sheet on which basic data are recorded in the field. This usually consists of an indication as to which bones are present or absent, with the orientation and position of the skeleton in the ground and any other information which it is thought might be of use to the specialist. This may include measurement of the stature of the burial, but this information is not of much use to the specialist who will subsequently study the skeleton. Much more useful are the careful collection, labelling and storage of the burials so that the specialist's work is not hindered unnecessarily.

If an archaeologist wishes to do some primary analysis on a group of burials, then it is necessary to learn not only the bones but also the techniques of recording and analysing the information they contain. Examples of recording sheets used by the author are reproduced here (fig. 13); four are used for each skeleton. These are sheets that are used in the laboratory and not in the field, where it would be impossible to undertake this kind of analysis. While careful recording of the burials and their associations can and should be undertaken in the field, the detailed analysis implied in these forms should largely be undertaken by a specialist.

As can be seen from the sheets, there are various measurements that can be taken on the skeleton. Sheet 1 records first the number and state of the teeth and then the skeletal bones recovered. Sheet 2 shows in the mid-section the major measurements of the skull and mandible, and sheet 3 those of the long bones and the sexing of the individuals. Sheet 4 records the

Fig. 13a. Specialist recording sheet 1.

TEETH   1.

PERIOD	REF. NUMBER	MUSEUM	LOCALITY	SEX SKULL:	PELVIS: OTHER:
Anglo Saxon	H134	Anyvault	Anywhere	M	M M

ARCHAEOLOGICAL REFS. 0327 Level 1

LAB. REFS. HB7

AGE AT DEATH:
SUTURES — ADULT   TEETH — 25-35   PUBIC — 23-35

DEFORMATION: ANTE MORTEM/POST MORTEM

1
8 7 6 5 4 3 2 1   1 2 3 4 5 6 7 8 (R / L)
2 A C

R e d c b a   a b c d e L
e d c b a   a b c d e
(deciduous)

NP (permanent) 3 E   NP
4
Symbols -
CA = Congenital absence
x = Loss A.M.
/ = Loss P.M.
A = Abscess
E = Exposure of pulp
C = Caries
U = Unerupted
O = Erupting
NP = Not present

CARIES 2, 7/1/1/2 ; 3, 6/1/1/4

ABSCESSES 2, 6/1/4/0

PERIODONTAL DISEASE 2

CALCULUS 2

BITE O
Over-bite
Edge-to-edge
Under-bite

TOOTH ROTATION

OTHER DENTAL ANOMALIES

HYPOPLASIA Event at 3 years ± 12 months

ATTRITION Brothwell = 25-35

	M1	M2	M3
GRADE	4	3+	2+
PATTERN Upper = U Lower = L	U L	U L	U L

BONES PRESENT		Left	Right		Left	Right
SKULL ✓	MANUBRIUM	✓		PELVIS	✓	—
MANDIBLE ✓	STERNUM	✓		FEMUR	✓	—
VERTEBRAE:	CLAVICLE	✓	✓	PATELLA		—
C 7	SCAPULA	✓	✓	TIBIA	✓	—
T 12	RIBS	9	6	FIBULA	✓	—
L 5	HUMERUS	✓	✓	TARSALS	4	1
S 5	RADIUS	✓	✓	METATARSALS	3	1
Co 1	ULNA	✓	✓	FOOT PHALANGES	4	6
	CARPALS	5	3			
	METACARPALS	5	2			
	HAND PHALANGES	12	8			

Fig. 13b. Specialist recording sheet 2.

PERIOD Anglo Saxon	REF. NUMBER H134	MUSEUM Anyvault	LOCALITY Anywhere	CRANIAL	2.

SUTURE OBLITERATION	SPEN. W. Clear	CORONAL Clear	SAGITTAL Fading posteriorally	OCCIPITAL Clear

WORMIAN BONES	CORONAL /	SAGITTAL /	LAMBDOID 4 on R 2 on L	INCA. B. /

METOPISM Complete suture retained	PARIETAL NOTCH B. R = 1 L = 0	ORBITAL OSTEOPOROSIS R = 4 L = 4

TORUS MANDIB.	AUDITIVUS /	PALATIVUS Slight	MAXILLARIS /

PARIETAL FORAM. Paired	SPHEN. ARTIC 1	EPIPTERIC BONES Both sides	SUP. ORB. FORAM Both complete

GLAB.OCCIP.L.(L)	190 mm	MAX.B. PYRIF.AP.(NB)	23 mm
MAX.BI-PARIETAL.B.(B)	141	NASAL HT.(HN)	50
MIN.FRONT.B.(B)	103	AURICULAR HT.(OH)	120
BASIO-BREG.HT.(H)	131	BREG.AURIC HT.(BOH)	116
BAS-NASION L.(LB)	106	SIMOTIC CH (SC)	12
NAS-BREG.ARC.(S_1)	118	BI-DAC CH(DC)	23
BREG-LAMBDA ARC (S_2)	123	BIASTER.BR.(BLAST.B)	125
LMDA-OPISTH.ARC(S_3)	122	BI-CONDYLAR WIDTH (W_1)	125
TOTAL SAG.ARC(S)	366	CONDYLE LENGTH (CyL)	71
TRANSVERSE BREG.ARC.(T^1)	290	RAMUS B.(least)(RB)	32
HORIZ.CIRCUM.(U)	535	SAGIT.HT.MANDIB.(H_1)	28
NAS-BREG.CHORD(S^1)	109	FORAM.MENTALIA B.(ZZ)	50
BREG-LMDA.CH.(S_2)	110	CORONAL B.(CrCr)	97
LMDA-OPISTH.CH.(S_3)	95	MANDIBULAR ANGLE(MZ)	120°
NAS-ALVEOL.LGTH.(G'H)	67	BI-GONIAL BREADTH (GoGo)	104
BAS-ALVEOL.LGTH.(GL)	99	MAX PROJ.L.MANDIB.(ML)	107
FACIAL BREADTH (GB)	96	CORONOID HT.(CrH)	94
PALATE B.(2nd M)(G_2)	38	HEIGHT AT 2ND MOLAR (M_2H)	38
PALATE LENGTH (G'3)	47	MASTOID L	37
MAX.ZYGOM.B.(J)	133	TOTAL FACIAL HT.	119
ORBITAL B.(O_1)	40	CRANIAL INDEX	74.2 = Dolicho cranic
HT.OF L.ORBIT(O_2)	32		
FORAMINAL L.(FL)	29		
FORAMINAL B.(FB)	31		

NON-METRICAL CRANIAL TRAITS

CRANIAL PATHOLOGIES

Healed porotic hyperostosis on both parietals and superior portion of occipital.

Fig. 13c. Specialist recording sheet 3.

PERIOD	REF. NUMBER	MUSEUM	LOCALITY	LONGBONES	3.
Anglo Saxon	H 134	Anyvault	Anywhere	SEXING	

FEMUR	LEFT	RIGHT	HUMERUS	LEFT	RIGHT	STATURE
MAXL. FeL$_1$	441 mm		MAX.L.HUL$_1$	317 mm	315 mm	Bone = Fem+Tib
OBLIQUE L. FeL$_2$	440		MAX.DIAM.HUD$_1$	21	24	Sex = M
TROCHANT L. FeL$_3$	425		MIN.DIAM.HUD$_2$	18	21	Over 30 = ?
MIN.A.P.DIAM.FeD$_1$	284		MIN. CIRCUM.	—	—	166·25 ± 2·99
TRANSVERSE " FeD$_2$	332		Diam. Hd.	50	49	= 5' 5½" ±1·2"
DIAM. HEAD.	49					
A.P.DIAM.MIDSHAFT	28·9		RADIUS			REFS.
M.L. " "	28·9		MAX.L.RaL$_4$	227	226	
CIRCUMFERENCE MIDSHAFT	92					Trotter and
BICONDYLAR W.	84		ULNA			Gleser
ROBUSTICITY INDEX	13·1		MAX.L. ULL$_1$	246	245	
TIBIA			PLATYMERIA	85.5		
MAX.L.TIL$_1$	351 mm					
OBLIQUE L. TIL$_2$	343		PLATYCNEMIA	84.3		
MAX.A.P.DIAM.TID$_1$	313					
TRANSVERSE DIAM.TID$_2$	264					
BICONDYLAR W.T$_1$E$_1$	85		SACRUM			
FIBULA			LENGTH			
			BREADTH			
MAX.L. FiL$_1$	343		INDEX			

OTHER (SPECIFY)

SEXING:

PELVIS:

1) SCIATIC NOTCH:

DEEP = ✓   ANGLE =
SHALLOW =   CHORDS =

2) PRE-AURICULAR SULCUS:
   PRESENT =
   ABSENT = ✓

3) OBTURATOR FORAMEN:
   OVOID = ✓
   TRIANGULAR =

CRANIUM:

1) POSTERIOR ROOT OF ZYGOMATIC PROCESS:
   EXTENDED AND WELL-DEFINED = ✓
   NOT " " " " =

2) SUPRA-ORBITAL RIDGE:
   LARGE = ✓
   SMALL =

3) NUCHAL CREST:
   LARGE = ✓
   SMALL =

Fig. 13d. Specialist recording sheet 4.

PERIOD	REF. NUMBER	MUSEUM	LOCALITY	AGEING 4.
Anglo Saxon	H134	Anyvault	Anywhere	NON-METRICS PATHOLOGIES CONCLUSIONS

EPIPHYSEAL CLOSURE:	FULLY FUSED	PARTLY FUSED	UNFUSED	AGE
FEMUR	✓			All adult
TIBIA	✓			
FIBULA	✓			
CLAVICE	✓			
HUMERUS	✓			
RADIUS	✓			
ULNA	✓			
PELVIS = ILIAC =	✓			
ISCHIAL =	✓			
VERTEBRAE = BODY =	✓			
PROCESSES =	✓			✓
RIBS =	✓			

POST-CRANIAL NON-METRICS

C4 has bipartite transverse forams.
Femur has an Allen's fossa and a third
trochanter.
Tibia has a squatting facet.

PUBIC SYMPHYSEAL AGEING

COMPONENT I	= 23
" II	= 26
" III	= 35

PATHOLOGIES

L. Tibia and fibula have old, healed spiral fractures (see X-ray).
T8–12 inclusive have Schmorl's nodes, and marginal anterior osteophytes.
Bilateral os acromiale.
All long bones strong and robust with well developed muscle insertions.

CONCLUSIONS An adult male, probably in his late 20s/early 30s. About
5' 5" tall, with evidence for childhood iron deficiency anaemia. There
is an old fracture of the left leg and a stressed back which may
be related to occupation. The os acromiale suggests considerable shoulder
stresses.

observations from which the age, physical and medical history of the individual may be deduced. For an explanation of these measurements and how to take them see the books by Brothwell (1981) and Bass (1971). Analysis of the many cranial measurements will suggest to the specialist the similarities and differences within a population which will be of interest, particularly at certain periods when there were changes in head shape from one form to another. This kind of analysis will also suggest what the people looked like, whether, for example, they had long, narrow faces or square chins, what shape their eye sockets were and so on. Also included on sheet 2 in the top section is a series of boxes for non-metrical (not measured) traits, features that can be scored as present or absent. They include, for example, a series of extra bones which may be included in the cranial sutures and other special features which are apparent to the observer. Non-metrical traits also occur in the post-cranial skeleton. They are often considered to suggest genetic relationships, with the possibility that some of them at least will be shared by members of a family. For a complete description of these traits, see the papers by Berry and Berry (1967) and Finnegan (1978).

The data on sheet 3 will allow the calculation of adult stature, using the long bone measurements and certain formulae calculated by Trotter (1970). Other indices may also be calculated from the diameters of the shafts of the long bones.

One of the main tasks of the specialist is the aging and sexing of human skeletal material. The former is easier the younger the individuals, while the latter is only possible with any degree of accuracy with adults.

Sexing of adults

There are differences between the two sexes that are displayed on adult skeletons and that are related to the different functions of those skeletons. Identifying the various characteristics of sexual dimorphism depends on those characteristics being clearly displayed. Generally they are, but in every group of skeletons there are one or two that are very difficult or even impossible to sex, since they do not possess the necessary characteristics in a clearly defined manner. Also it is possible to sex with any security only if the relevant bones survive, and occupation may well affect the robusticity and muscularity of an individual, producing problems with sexing. One can imagine, for example, the problems to be encountered with attempts to sex the skeletons of some athletes.

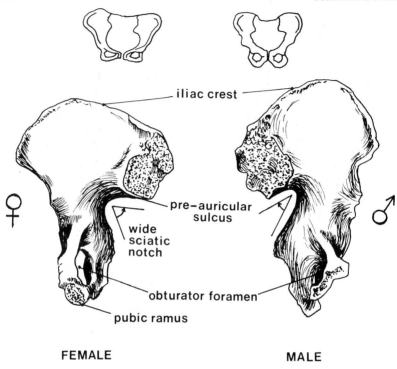

Fig. 14. Sexing in the pelvis. The features illustrated differentiate the sexes. (After Brothwell, 1981.)

The bones which have the clearest sexual differences are those of the pelvis and the skull, particularly the former. The female pelvis is both shallower and broader than the male, since it is necessary both to support, and subsequently to pass, a foetus through it (fig. 14). This broadening leads to an elongation of the pubic ramus, producing a sub-pubic angle of more than 90 degrees. There is also an elongation at the sacro-iliac articulation, which often gives rise to a wide, shallow sciatic notch, and a preauricular sulcus or groove just below the articulations. The obturator foramen tends to be more triangular in shape in the female. Conversely, the male pelvis has a higher, narrower, more S-shaped iliac crest, a shorter, steeper pubic ramus, with a sub-pubic angle of less than 90 degrees, a deeper sciatic notch and generally no pre-auricular sulcus or groove.

The male skull has areas that are more pronounced and developed than in the female skull (fig. 15). At the sides and rear of the skull are areas for the attachment of various muscles, which tend to be more developed in the male. Thus at the very rear of the skull there is a more developed nuchal crest and there are larger mastoid bones behind both the ears. The zygomatic arch extends beyond the opening for the ear-hole and there is a more developed supra-orbital or brow-ridge. The frontal bone or forehead tends to slope more in the male, whereas in the female it is straighter and steeper. The underlined areas on fig. 15 will help to clarify these points. These changes occur gradually during the pubescent years, in the skeleton and in soft tissue, and this is why it is impossible to sex the skeletons of young children and very difficult even with adolescents.

Aging of skeletons

It is very much easier to age children and adolescents than it is to age adults. The growth that occurs during childhood and adolescence also affects the skeleton. This is most apparent in the eruption of the deciduous and then the permanent teeth. As can be seen from fig. 16 this occurs within set time scales, so that a child can be aged relatively closely. The gradual increase in size

Fig. 15. Sexing in the skull. The underlined areas differentiate the sexes. (After Bass, 1971.)

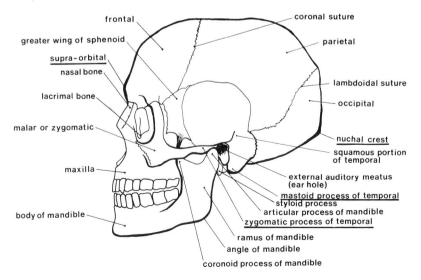

frontal
coronal suture
greater wing of sphenoid
parietal
supra-orbital
nasal bone
lacrimal bone
lambdoidal suture
occipital
malar or zygomatic
nuchal crest
squamous portion of temporal
maxilla
external auditory meatus (ear hole)
mastoid process of temporal
styloid process
articular process of mandible
zygomatic process of temporal
body of mandible
ramus of mandible
angle of mandible
coronoid process of mandible

32

Human Bones

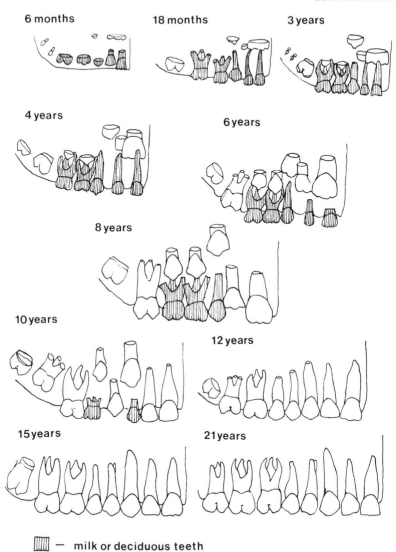

▥ — milk or deciduous teeth

Fig. 16. Human tooth eruption. (After Brothwell, 1981.)

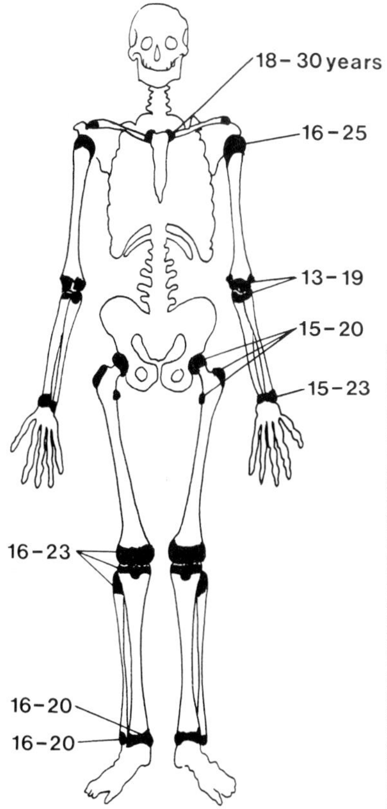

Fig. 17. *(Left).* Epiphyseal union. (After Brothwell, 1981.)

18 – 30 years

16 – 25

13 – 19

15 – 20

15 – 23

16 – 23

16 – 20

16 – 20

Plate 3. An unfused epiphysis. The humerus (upper arm bone) on the right has an unfused epiphysis.

of the bones of the skeleton is obtained because many of them have growing ends or *epiphyses*. These epiphyses are held in place by plates of cartilage, thus allowing the main body of the bone to continue growth. Fig. 17 shows the age ranges during which these epiphyses unite with the main part of the bone, the cartilaginous plate becoming ossified. There are a number of skeletons from the *Mary Rose* with unfused epiphyses, suggesting the presence of adolescents on the ship (plate 3).

The aging of adult remains is much more difficult, especially after the age of twenty-five years, when all the teeth are usually erupted and all the epiphyses fused. The method that is most widely utilised is that of attrition patterns or wear on the permanent molars, if they survive. Brothwell (1981) and Miles (1963) have calculated age ranges based on these patterns. This work, however, has been done only for pre-medieval and Anglo-Saxon British groups, and so has limited application for later groups, where there may have been a drastic change in diet.

Another method which may be used is that of age-related changes occurring at the pubic symphysis (where the two pelvic bones meet). McKern and Stewart (1957) and Gilbert and McKern (1973) have established standards for males and females respectively which are of use.

It is important to emphasise that any method of sexing or aging human skeletal remains must be used with caution, since all have their limitations. It is also important to understand that in the case of aging only an age range may be produced with any degree of confidence, not an absolute age.

4
Pathology

The whole problem of palaeopathology is one that is best left to the expert, although some general descriptive remarks may be made that will be of interest and may be of some use.

Diagnosis of pathology is always difficult, even in the living, when at least there is a patient to say where it hurts. For example, the success rate of firm diagnosis of arthritis in modern clinical practice is accepted by some specialists as less than 25 per cent (Dieppe, 1983). Diagnosis in dry bone is even more difficult, particularly when a skeleton may well be incomplete or even fragmentary.

A problem for the non-specialist is differentiating between genuine and pseudo pathology and between ante-mortem and post-mortem conditions. There is often an overlap between the two, so that post-mortem damage may appear as pathology to the unwary or inexperienced. A good working rule that helps to overcome this problem is that if an area of damage shows no healing the causative event must have occurred at, or after, death. In the case of apparent fractures of the ribs, for example, the difference between the pseudo and the genuine case may be clearly seen by looking at plate 4, where the true fracture shows healing and the formation of a supporting framework of callus, all of which must have occurred in life and which do not appear on the rib which has suffered post-mortem damage. On the other hand, in the case of a decapitation, which may have been the cause of death, the cutting marks on the base of the skull or on the cervical vertebrae will look fresh and unhealed. It is not possible to say whether the decapitation occurred just before, at, or fairly soon after death.

Living bone is covered by a membrane of connective tissue called the *periosteum*, which covers all the bone except for the joint surfaces, which are covered by cartilage. This periosteum, because it is a living tissue, is reactive, responding to any external attacks on the bone by disease or accident and, although it does not persist in dry bone, the effects of this response do and are known as *periosteal reaction*. This reaction serves to emphasise another characteristic of living bone: that, although it appears so hard and stable, it is very plastic and responds in a variety of ways to every event, whether long-term, such as changes which may be related to occupation, or traumatic, as in the case of a fracture.

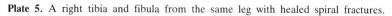

Plate 4. Pseudo and true pathology. The shorter rib has a healed fracture; the longer rib was broken after death.

Plate 5. A right tibia and fibula from the same leg with healed spiral fractures.

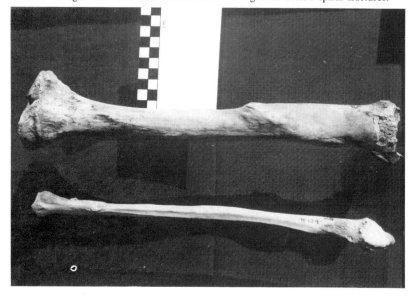

There is constant modelling during the growing period and re-modelling occurs after any traumatic event, although the degree of this remodelling depends on the age of the individual. (Watt, 1984). The results of this activity may be seen, for example, in the skeleton of an old-fashioned blacksmith or of a professional weightlifter, where the bones will be very strong and robust, with very well developed insertions for the attaching tendons or ligaments. Varying degrees of this development occur on the bones from the *Mary Rose,* as can be seen in plate 1. Equally, remodelling after trauma can be seen in the case of healed fractures of the tibia and fibula from the *Mary Rose* (plate 5).

There are various diseases which are caused by the deficiency of certain vital nutrients in the diet and which leave their mark on the skeleton. Perhaps the best known of these is rickets, caused by a lack of vitamin D. This vitamin is found in certain foods such as fish oils, and is synthesised by the action of sunlight on the skin. Although rickets does occur in the archaeological record, it became particularly prevalent during the industrial revolution, when the combination of very poor diet and severe overcrowding in the closely packed cities led to its increase. Porotic hyperostosis of the cranium (plate 6) and osteoporosis of the upper orbits (plate 7) are both thought to be related to a deficiency of dietary iron, causing anaemia in childhood. The effects of these deficiencies are, however, retained in the skeleton because of the plasticity of the bone. A lack of vitamin C, which produces scurvy in as short a time as four to six weeks in the adult, may also affect the skeleton, but it is difficult to diagnose in dry bone since its main effects are on the soft tissues.

A possible case of rickets from the *Mary Rose* is shown in plate 8, although an alternative explanation is that this may have been a growth anomaly, since there is normally a variation in the amount of bowing of the tibia (Gallant, 1984). This point emphasises one of the major problems for the palaeopathologist, that it is often very difficult to diagnose a specific condition and to differentiate one pathology from another. This is much easier with many congenital but non-pathological conditions, such as a retained metopic suture in the frontal bone of the cranium (plate 9), or the presence of a hidden spina bifida occulta in the sacrum (plate 10). There are various genetic disorders in the pattern of growth which are a function of too early or too late union of the epiphyses and which give rise to dwarfism and to giantism respectively. There are other congenital disorders which are

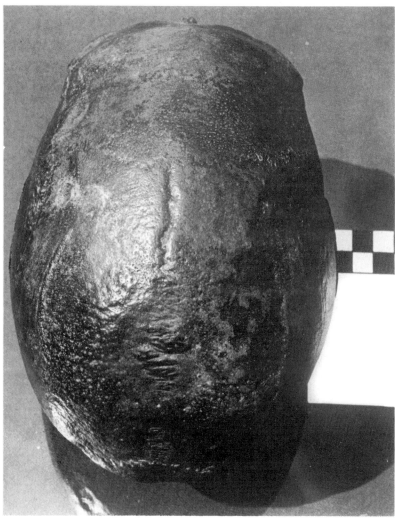

Plate 6. Porotic hyperostosis of the cranium. The top of the skull is very pitted and bumpy in appearance.

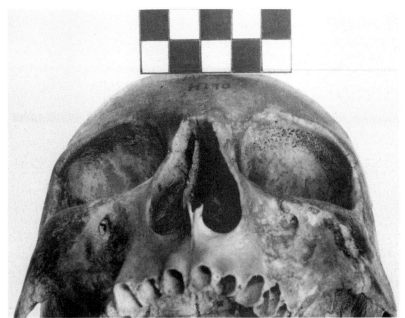

Plate 7. *(Above).* Osteoporosis of the upper orbits. The tops of the eye sockets are pitted.

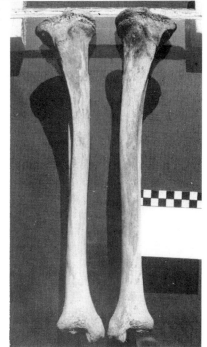

Plate 8. *(Right).* Possible rickets in a pair of tibia. Both tibia are bowed outwards, particularly towards the top.

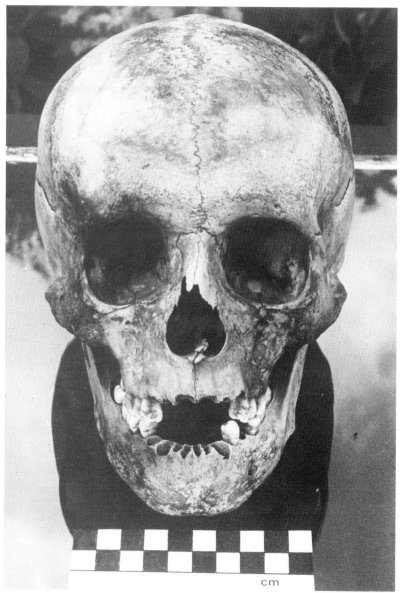

Plate 9. Retained metopic suture. The line running up the front of the skull is the suture.

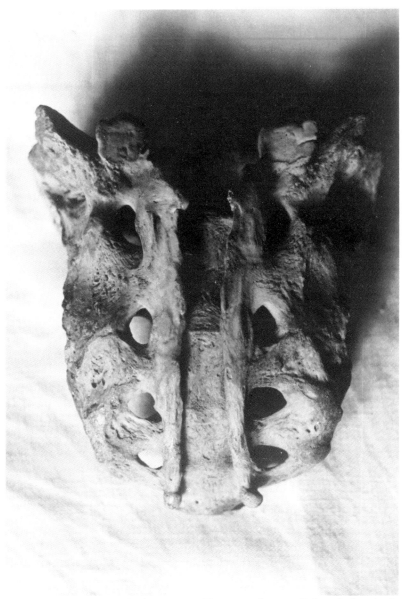

Plate 10. Spina bifida occulta in a sacrum. The sacrum is open all down its length; the vertebrae should be closed at the mid-line.

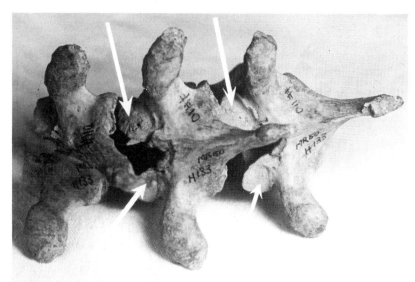

Plate 11. *(Above)*. Arthritic changes in vertebral articular surfaces. There is pitting of the flat articular surfaces of these thoracic vertebrae (arrows).

Plate 12. *(Left)*. Tuberculosis of the spine. This spine is fused from the lumber segment upwards and permanently bent at an angle of about 90 degrees. The person was, however, living with this condition.

apparent in the skeleton, such as bilateral dislocation of the hip, nowadays treated by placing the new-born infant in a frog splint for the first few months of its life. Other disorders produce deformities of the skull, although these can also be artificially induced, either in life by such techniques as cradle-board flattening, or after death, by the weight of the soil overburden.

The most common pathology encountered in an archaeological context is that associated with arthritic changes. These may be traumatic or degenerative in nature (plate 11). Other common pathological conditions are various kinds of fractures. Long-term disease, such as syphilis, leprosy or tuberculosis, will affect the skeleton, the last two with more frequency than the first (Hackett, 1984). The effects of diseases such as these can be very dramatic, as can be seen from plate 12. For those readers who wish to pursue this interesting topic further there are excellent texts by Steinbock (1976), Ortner and Putschar (1981) and Manchester (1983).

The most important contribution to be made to the field of palaeopathology by archaeologists today is not in the accuracy of their diagnoses, but rather in the careful and meticulous description of each case, whether it can be diagnosed or not, supported by good photographs and, where possible, radiographs. In this way an adequate record is kept for future workers, who may have the advantage of better diagnostic techniques and a greater knowledge of the subject.

5
Cremations

Valuable information can be obtained from a study of cremated human bones as well as from inhumed burials. The amount and quality of such information will depend on the nature of the ritual used, the manner of burning and the subsequent burial conditions. It is often possible to obtain a considerable amount of evidence from groups of cremations, using the same anthropological techniques as for inhumations, suitably adapted.

The amount of evidence to be gained from a group of cremations depends largely on the size and nature of the surviving fragments. There is a great deal of variability in the quantity and the quality of this evidence, depending on the period from which the material comes, the techniques used for burning and whether the bone was subsequently broken into uniform fragments for insertion into an urn or other container for burial. Inurned bone, whether the urn survives intact or not, is often in a better condition than bone which has merely been inserted into a grave.

In the distant past, the ritual would be affected by the availability of suitable timber and by the weather. After the end of the bronze age and for the last two and a half to three thousand years, the climate has been colder and damper than it had previously been. Many cremation fires must have been summarily quenched by the inevitable downpour, thus producing poorly burnt bone. As will be seen, other factors may also have affected the degree of burning achieved.

The efficient techniques that are used in modern cremation, at least in the western world, will prevent future anthropologists from obtaining any information from the ashes. Plates 13 and 14 show the relative inefficiency of the bronze age techniques, and a great deal of information can therefore be obtained from them (Clay, 1981). While it is fairly unusual for whole sections of spine to survive burning, (plate 14), the material shown in plate 13, which is from the primary burial in the group, shows the nature of many surviving bones, at least from this period.

The most commonly surviving fragments are from the long bones and the cranium although, depending on the position of the fire, finger and foot phalanges may also survive and often the crowns of teeth. A careful record of surviving fragments should be made, and Janet Henderson of the Ancient Monuments Laboratory has very kindly allowed me to reproduce the

Plate 13. Cremation from Sproxton, Leicestershire. The primary burial from this barrow.

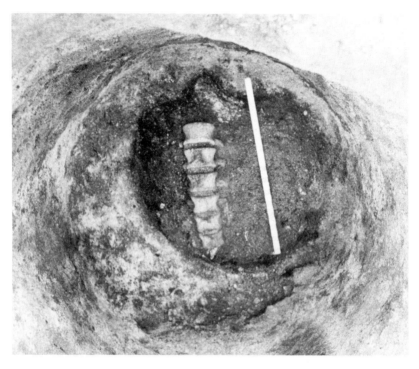

Plate 14. Cremation from Sproxton, Leicestershire. A partially burnt spine.

recording form which she uses for this purpose (fig. 18).

After careful sieving and analysis of all the fragments they should be weighed, since the more complete the individual, particularly when it is an adult, the heavier the cremation. The temperature of burning affects not only the survival of the fragments but also their colour. Bone burnt at a high temperature is white in colour and more twisted, cracked and heavily calcined than that burnt at a lower temperature, which is either merely charred or blue and less cracked and twisted in appearance.

The author was involved with the analysis of two important bronze age barrow groups from Leicestershire (Clay, 1981), which illustrate the kind of information to be obtained from cremations and the problems associated with work on them. Both were multiphase barrows which were used by a community over a long period and it is possible that different rituals and methods of cremation may have been used in each (Clay, 1981, page 47). In the case of the larger group, from Sproxton, the ritual may well

Notes for Cremated Human Skeletal Remains

Site: __Anywhere__   Burial no. __H 123__

Period: __Anytime__   AML no. __4 - 567 - 8 AML__

Observer: __Anyone__   Date: __29/7/86__

Colour: White, calcined.

Identified Bone: Cranium
                     Tooth crowns/roots
                     Femur
                     Pelvis
                     Phalanges (hand)
                     Long bones

No. of Individuals: 1

Age: Adult

Sex: ? M

Stature: N.P.

Anomalies/Pathology: Porotic Hyperostosis of cranium and orbital roof, (both)

Maximum Length: 155 mm

Weights: 1.5 kg

Other: None

Fig. 18. Cremation recording form.

have included a period of defleshing of the body, probably by exposure on a burial platform, before cremation. This ritual was possibly associated with economic necessity. If individuals died at an inconvenient time when everyone was very busy, what was undoubtedly a complex and extended riual could not be easily undertaken. In this case the body may well have been left exposed on a platform or in a mortuary house until the community was free to dispose of it with all due ceremony. Such exposure would mean that putrefaction or carrion might remove the soft tissues, while the bones remained in place since the body was off the ground and away from animal scavengers. While such practices may seem distasteful, these early groups of agricultural-ists were at the mercy of the environment and the climate in a way which is difficult for us to understand. We have only to consider the effects of a drought or a late growing season in parts of the world on the subsistence patterns, lifestyles and rituals of certain groups, to imagine how similar events could have affected life in the bronze age. The cremation ritual at Sproxton seems to have involved a method where the body, in whatever form it was burnt, was laid on the ground, possibly in a shallow scoop or pit, rather than being placed on a pyre. This is inferred because there appears to have been a variation in the efficiency of the fire and the nature and condition of the surviving bone fragments (Clay, 1981, page 19).

The other group, from Eaton in Leicestershire, is smaller and very different in nature. In this case the bone is very blackened and stained, (Clay, 1981, page 41), suggesting that these individuals may have been cremated while flesh and blood were still present (Brothwell, 1981, page 16). These two groups from Leicestershire, therefore, exhibit some of the features and some of the problems to be encountered in the study of cremated human bone.

The cremation of human beings for research is not allowed but some experimental work has been done on animal carcases. This is an area in which more information is needed. The most closely related animal available is the pig, and the experimental burning of portions of pig carcase under controlled conditions should yield much useful information on temperatures of burning, subsequent appearance of the bone and so on.

6
Some interesting cases

The day-to-day study of groups of excavated skeletons constantly increases our knowledge of ancient diet, pathology and lifestyles, and interesting and unusual cases sometimes emerge. For instance, when there is pathology present in a skeleton, specialists may disagree as to its diagnosis. Some conditions are easier to diagnose than others, while with some a positive diagnosis is not possible. Even when diagnosis is possible, the interpretation of the causative event may lead to disagreement. An example of this is the Roman practice of decapitation.

Decapitations

Small numbers of beheadings occur in some of the larger groups of skeletons from the Roman period in Britain. For example, Wells found at least six decapitations at the large Roman cemetery at Cirencester, Gloucestershire, and ten were found at Dunstable, Bedfordshire. There are a number in the group of about 280 Roman burials from Ashton, Northamptonshire. All these cemeteries were in use during the third and fourth centuries AD.

It is not possible in the case of decapitation to say whether it is the cause of death or a post-mortem ritual associated with a small number of individuals. As has already been shown, no healing or remodelling of the bone occurs. It has been assumed both at Cirencester and at Dunstable, however, that the beheadings were punitive in nature and, therefore, the cause of death. At Cirencester one woman had been beheaded and six women were similarly treated at Dunstable. At Ashton, one of the possible decapitations is of a child and there is a beheaded baby at Dunstable. It seems unlikely that these beheadings, at least, were punitive.

At both Ashton and Dunstable the heads appear to have been severed and then buried away from the neck, while at Cirencester they seem to have usually been buried in the normal position, so that the decapitations were discovered only when the neck bones were examined and cuts were detected. It is assumed, therefore, that in this case the soft tissues at the front of the neck remained intact, thus holding the head in place. It is probable from the nature of the cuts in these three examples that the beheadings were done with very sharp weapons, since there are only one or two clean cuts in every case. Some of the cuts are very high on the neck. The nature and position of the cuts suggest an alternative interpretation to the punitive one. If the individual was already dead it would be possible to inflict the cut quickly, cleanly and in any position on the neck, without damage to other vertebrae.

A search of the historical literature reveals no evidence for the widespread use of decapitation as a form of capital punishment. The preferred method throughout the Roman Empire would appear to have been crucifixion, although stoning, stabbing and poisoning were also used. Of these, only crucifixion would possibly leave evidence on the skeleton. The fact remains, however, that in Britain there are small groups of decapitated men, women and children within some Roman cemeteries. They present an interesting anomaly that is difficult to explain. Although some would argue that they are penal groups, the author's view is that the evidence equally points to a post-mortem ritual practised on a few, or special, individuals.

Various diseases

Cases in which an individual has suffered from a congenital condition such as spina bifida may persist in the archaeological record. These are extremely rare, however, since the expectation of post-natal life for such individuals was very low. Evidence for infectious disease such as tuberculosis has already been mentioned in the example from Elstow Abbey, Bedfordshire (see plate 12). There are further examples of this disease and of other diseases such as leprosy and poliomyelitis. For example, an apparent case of poliomyelitis has been reported in an adult male from Dunstable, Bedfordshire, and there is another probable case from Raunds, Northamptonshire.

Another disease which has appeared infrequently in the record is gout. An example has been diagnosed in a group from Missenden Abbey, Buckinghamshire. This was a group of four adult males who were buried at the crossing of the abbey church in a position of some importance archaeologically. On examination, it was apparent that one of the older men in the group had gout affecting his feet, particularly on the right. This disease is due to a metabolic disorder which causes an excess of uric acid to enter the bloodstream. It then becomes deposited in the joints as uric acid crystals. These in turn erode the bone, producing lesions (plates 15 and 16). They also produce spicules called tophi which grow into the soft tissue, causing swelling, inflammation and pain. If an individual has the necessary metabolic disorder and a

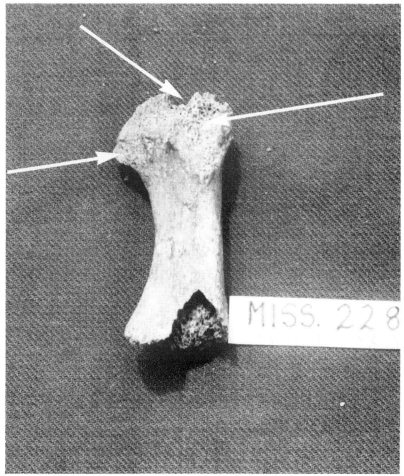

Plate 15. Gout. There are classic 'punched-out' lytic lesions visible on the first right metatarsal (arrows).

diet high in the production of uric acid, gout may result. The disease affects a few individuals, mostly men from middle age onwards, and has traditionally been associated with a rich diet. The Missenden Abbey case is aged thirty-five to forty-five years and, it is considered by the excavator, is part of a small group of socially important individuals, because of the position of burial. He was presumably a man who could afford to eat well.

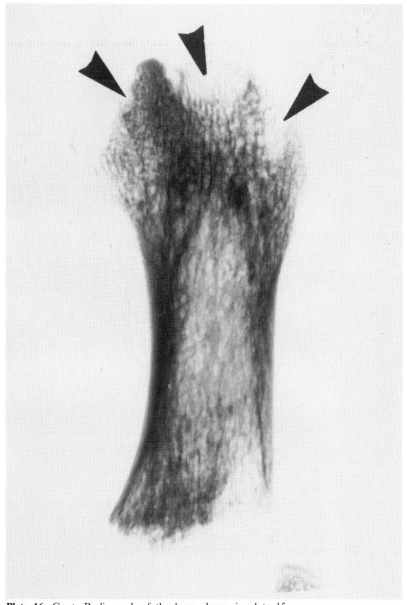

Plate 16. Gout. Radiograph of the bone shown in plate 15.

Occupational related pathology : the Mary Rose site

Prolonged physical activity of particular kinds will induce changes in the skeleton. It is easy to understand that a lifetime of very hard physical work such as mining, or intensive physical activity such as gymnastics, will eventually have an effect on the skeleton. This is especially true if the activity has been practised, as was often the case in the past, from a relatively early age, when the individual was still growing. Possible changes in the skeleton related to activity or occupation are an interesting study. It is usually very difficult to evaluate such changes in archaeological groups of skeletons. Firstly, although the archaeologist may consider that there are good *terminus ante* and *post quem* dates for the use of a cemetery, this does not tell us when the burials were interred within that timespan. For example, a cemetery may have been used over three hundred years and have three hundred burials. It is not possible to say whether all were buried during one century or less, or whether they are spaced out over time in a random fashion. Secondly, the specific occupations practised by a group of people are very rarely known. Even if there is good archaeological retrieval of artefacts and working floors, it is often impossible to say when specific occupations were actually followed during the given timespan. This is a fundamental archaeological dilemma. Relating artefacts and people to specific events and points in time is usually impossible. There are always too many variables and unknown factors.

These limitations do not exist with the crew of the *Mary Rose*. Not only is the precise date of death known (19th July 1545) but there is also a record of their occupations in the Anthony Roll (Rule, 1982, page 27). This represents a unique opportunity, therefore, to study the activity or occupationally related pathological changes that may have happened to these men.

The analysis of the surviving skeletal remains suggests that the men were predominantly in the age range eighteen to twenty-five years, with a stature range of 5 feet 3 inches to 6 feet (1.6 to 1.8 m), largely strong and robust of build, exactly what would be expected for a group of fighting men. The conditions aboard the ship appear to have been such that most men probably had reasonable headroom in which to live and work. However the environment was unstable in comparison with a modern ship, since there was only a shallow keel and relatively little ballast. There are changes in some of the thigh bones which may be a reflection of this instability, particularly as many of the men would have been in this environment while still growing.

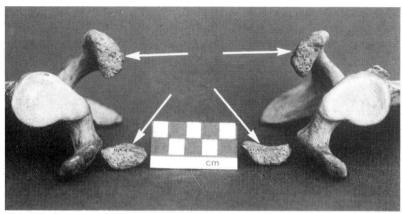

Plate 17. Os acromiale. The epiphysis at the end of the acromion of both scapulae (shoulder blades) is not fused, and the false joint surface is pitted and reactive (arrows). (Photograph: D. J. Stirland.)

One of the known occupations is that of archer or longbowman. Large numbers of bows and arrows have been recovered from the ship, as well as other archery equipment. Throughout the medieval period the English longbowman had been most successful, particularly against the French, and had been responsible for the victories of Crècy and Agincourt. Unlike the modern archer, who draws a relatively light short bow, his equivalent on the *Mary Rose* was drawing a heavy yew bow 6 feet (1.8 m) long. Draw weight is defined as the loading required to draw the string in order to fire the bow. The draw weight of most of these weapons was 125 pounds (56.7 kg). There were a small number of lighter bows with a draw weight of 80 pounds (36.3 kg), and three extremely heavy bows. To draw a bow of even 60 pounds weight puts a loading of about 300 pounds (136 kg) on each shoulder joint.

During the medieval period all males were required to learn to use a longbow (Trevelyan, 1967). They started at a very early age and the bows grew with them. In battle the longbow was used essentially as a saturation weapon, with between twelve and twenty arrows a minute being fired by each archer at a large target. This was almost certainly the method used with the heavier bows on the *Mary Rose*. The lighter bows would have been used as target weapons by skilled individual archers positioned as snipers in the rigging or fighting tops to pick off specific individuals on enemy ships. It is not clear how and for what particular targets the heaviest bows were used, although they may have fired burning pitch balls into the enemy's sails or rigging.

The persistent and long-term use of these weapons put considerable strains on growing skeletons, particularly in the shoulder regions. During study of the skeletal remains from the *Mary Rose,* an unusually high frequency of a very rare anomaly was recorded. This is a developmental defect in which the epiphysis at the end of the bar or acromial process across the back of the shoulder blade fails to unite (plate 17 and fig. 10). This non-fusion, it is argued, was encouraged by the persistent and long-term use of the heavy bows. In the shoulders from the *Mary Rose,* a false joint with a pitted, reactive surface was produced (indicated in the plate by arrows). It is suggested that the presence and frequency of the anomaly may indicate some of the archers in this group of skeletons.

Still births

The cover picture of a female skeleton shows the presence of a cluster of bones in the abdominal area and between the pelvic bones of the main skeleton. These small bones are the remains of a foetus still lying within the mother's body. It can be seen that the skull bones are at the top of the cavity and that the baby is lying in the classic breech position. This position presents hazards at birth even today and, in the past, must have been the cause of many still births and maternal deaths, as here.

Burial conditions

As was explained in chapter 1, burials in sand are often attacked and destroyed by the acidic conditions, leaving an empty grave. Excavations at Sutton Hoo emphasise this point. The outlines of two individuals had been detected by differences in the colour of the soil. After spraying with Vinamul, a hardening agent, the outlines were conserved, and the individuals could be excavated. One was raised and removed for further work, and the other remains in the ground (plate 18). They have become known as the 'sandmen'.

Historical individuals : the princes in the Tower

The human skeletal biologist may become involved in the attempted identification of specific historical figures from their supposed skeletal remains. Perhaps the most famous example of

Human Bones

Plate 18. Sandman. One of the
excavated 'inhumations' at Sutton Hoo. The body stain has
been fixed and hardened with
Vinamul and then blocked out.
(Photograph: D. J. Stirland.
Copyright: Sutton Hoo Re-
search Trust.)

this kind is the case of the princes in the Tower.

After Richard, Duke of York, the younger of the two sons of Edward IV, joined his brother, Edward V, in the Tower of London on 16th June 1483, neither of them was ever seen again outside the building. Their fate is unknown, but it has traditionally been assumed that they were murdered and that their uncle, who became King Richard III, was responsible for their deaths. In 1674 some bones were found by workmen under a staircase in the White Tower. These bones were assumed to be those of the princes and Charles II ordered them to be buried in an urn in Henry VII's chapel in Westminster Abbey. In July 1933 the urn was opened and a medical examination made of the surviving bones. The work was presented to the Society of Antiquaries by Lawrence Tanner and Professor William Wright in November 1933. At the end of his examination Professor Wright felt able to show that the evidence for the remains being those of the two princes was 'as conclusive as could be desired, and definitely more conclusive than could, considering everything, have reasonably been expected'. The evidence also supported the view that the princes must have died during Richard III's reign, given the age assigned to the bones.

After Tanner's and Wright's examination, the urn was resealed and so the bones themselves are not available for further examination. A careful reading of the report and its photographs in the light of modern knowledge, however, suggests that the identification of the two skeletons with the princes is by no means firm. The bones are undoubtedly those of two children, but it is not possible to sex them. The description of the dentition suggests that the two are nearer in age and probably younger than was thought in 1933. The older child appears to have been in the range eight to twelve years and the younger seven to eleven years. The description of the other evidence for aging given for the older child also suggests a ten or eleven year old. The most important point in all this is that the only true evidence we have is that these bones were buried before 1674. The fact that they were found buried deeply and with domestic refuse would suggest that they could have been much older than 1483 since, in archaeological terms, the greater the depth, the older the burial. On the other hand, there is no evidence to suggest that these burials were made during 1483 or earlier. They could have been there for less than one hundred years when discovered in 1674. The whole area of the Tower has been in permanent use for far longer than the last five hundred years, and various human bones have been found from time to time.

The skeletal and archaeological evidence for the identification of the bones found in 1674 with those of the two princes is, at best, inconclusive. This case illustrates how difficult it can sometimes be for the human skeletal biologist to analyse material objectively, when the historical pressures point to a diagnosis.

The case of Josef Mengele

A modern example of this pressure is the identification in Brazil of the remains of the Nazi war criminal Josef Mengele. The man concerned died and was buried under the name of Wolfgang Gerhard. He died by drowning in February 1979 and, when excavated in 1985, his body was already largely skeletonised. The entire skeleton was recovered, although much of it was broken (some during excavation), leached and eroded. Positive identification of modern skeletal material is often achieved through comparison of dental and medical records. In this case, since Mengele had been in hiding since 1945, there were no up-to-date records of this nature. The only existing dental records date from 1937-8. According to a dental specialist, however, three molars had fillings that corresponded to the records. While this skeleton could be sexed as an adult male, the problem of age was a difficult one. As has already been stated, the aging of adult remains becomes increasingly difficult with advancing age and Mengele would have been in his seventies. The pathologist who originally examined the body of the drowned man is reported as saying that this man was no more than about fifty-five years old. It was also suggested by experts that there was some evidence for an old hip injury which Mengele is supposed to have sustained as a young man.

The conclusions reached at the end of the examination were similar to those in the case of the princes. It was felt that, while the evidence was not conclusive, the body could have been that of Mengele. It must be remembered that there were considerable pressures, financial, political and social, for a positive diagnosis to be made.

7
Conclusion

The study of human skeletal remains can be of absorbing interest, and it is to be hoped that some of this interest has been conveyed. Once they are introduced to this area of archaeology, many people find it fascinating. Understandably, most non-specialists are unaware of the amount of information that can be obtained from human skeletal remains and of the contribution that this work may make to archaeology. Apart from any other considerations, the work of the palaeopathologist may contribute to forensic science, and the study of dietary deficiencies may have applications in the third world. Unlike any other field of archaeology, however, this work is involved with the remains of the people themselves, and it is in this that much of the fascination resides. Skeletons excavated from a burial ground belonged to ordinary people who had lived out their normal lifespan whatever that may have been. As ordinary people ourselves, there is great interest for us in this.

An examination of human evolution and of man's archaeological past is very exciting and it is of great importance that the ideas and results of this work should be freely conveyed to all who are interested. It should not be an elite and esoteric field of study that has no relevance for ordinary people. It is to be hoped that a knowledge and understanding of our past and the ordinary people who lived it , may help us to deal with the present and plan for a better future, when we will, ourselves, be archaeological relics.

8
Further reading

Bedfordshire Archaeological Journal, volume 15. The report on the burials from Dunstable.

Brothwell, D. R. *Digging Up Bones.* BMNH, Oxford University Press, 1981. A useful introductory text to the subject.

Current Archaeology, number 95. The report on the latest work at Sutton Hoo, including the 'sandmen'.

Cornwall, I. W. *Bones for the Archaeologist.* J. M. Dent and Sons, 1974. Compares human and animal bones.

Glob, P.V. *The Bog People.* Faber and Faber, 1973. A fascinating description of the bog burials of the Danish iron age.

Glob, P.V. *The Mound People.* Faber and Faber, 1974. This describes the earlier bronze age preserved burials in Denmark.

Manchester, Keith. *The Archaeology of Disease.* University of Bradford, 1983. An introduction to palaeopathology.

Ross, Charles. *Richard III.* Eyre Metheun, 1981.

Rule, Margaret. *The Mary Rose : The Excavation and Raising of Henry VIII's Flagship.* Windward, 1982.

Tanner, Lawrence E., and Wright, Professor William. 'Recent Investigations Regarding the Fate of the Princes in the Tower.' *Archaeologia,* volume 84, 1934. The account of the analysis of the bones from the urn in Henry VII's Chapel.

Trevelyan, G. M. *English Social History.* Pelican, 1967. Contains useful background information to some of the examples discussed.

References
The following is a list of technical publications referred to in the text. It is included for the benefit of those who might wish to pursue some more technical reading.

Bass, W. M. *Human Osteology : a Laboratory and Field Manual of the Human Skeleton.* Special Publications of the Missouri Archaeological Society, Columbia, Missouri, 1971.

Berry, A. C., and Berry R. J. 'Epigenetic Variation in the Human Cranium'. *Journal of Anatomy* 101, 2, 1967.

Clay, Patrick. *Two Multi-Phase Barrow Sites at Sproxton and Eaton, Leicestershire.* Leicestershire Museums, Art Galleries and Records Service, Archaeological Report Number 2, 1981.

Finnegan, M. 'Non-metric Variation of the Infracranial Skeleton'. *Journal of Anatomy* 125, 1, 1978.

Gilbert, B. M., and McKern, T. W. 'A Method for Ageing the Female Os Pubis'. *American Journal of Physical Anthropology* 38; Washington, 1973.

McKern, T. W., and Stewart T. D. *Skeletal Age Changes in Young American Males.* Technical Report, Headquarters Quartermaster Research and Development Command, Natick, Massachusetts, 1957.

Miles, A. E. W. *The Dentition in the Assessment of Individual Age in Skeletal Material.* Dental Anthropology, London, 1963.

Ortner, D. J., and Putschar, W. G. J. *Identification of Pathological Conditions in Human Skeletal Remains.* Smithsonian Contributions to Anthropology, Number 28. Washington, DC, 1981.

Steinbock, R. Ted. *Paleopathological Diagnosis and Interpretation.* Charles C. Thomas, 1976.

Trotter, Mildred. 'Estimation of Stature from Intact Long Limb Bones' in T. D. Stewart (editor) *Personal Identification in Mass Disasters.* Smithsonian Institution, Washington, DC, 1970.

9
Museums to visit

While there are skeletons in museums throughout Britain there are few skeletal collections on view to the public. Intending visitors to the museums listed below are advised to find out times of opening before making a special journey.

Dorset County Museum, High West Street, Dorchester, Dorset DT1 1XA. Telephone: Dorchester (0305) 62735. Some burials from Maiden Castle.
Hunterian Museum, Royal College of Surgeons of England, 35-43 Lincoln's Inn Fields, London WC2A 3PN. Telephone: 01-405 3474.
Science Museum, Exhibition Road, South Kensington, London SW7 2DD. Telephone: 01-589 3456. Houses the Wellcome Collection in which there is a small amount of human bone.
Wells Museum, 8 Cathedral Green, Wells, Somerset BA5 2UE. Telephone: Wells (0749) 73477. Material from Wells Cathedral.

Acknowledgements

I am particularly indebted to the published works of D. R. Brothwell and Dr W. M. Bass, and to Dr P. Dieppe, Dr M. Gallant and Dr I. Watt for many helpful comments. Many specialists in palaeopathology and related fields who have contributed are acknowledged in the text.

My personal thanks go to my husband, Derek Stirland, for all his help and critical encouragement. Thanks are also due to Steve Stringer for the photographic processing, and to Diedre O'Sullivan for permission to reproduce plate 2. I am most grateful to Leicestershire Museums for permission to reproduce plates 13 and 14, to the Sutton Hoo Research Trust for permission to reproduce plate 18, and to the Mary Rose Trust and Bedfordshire County Council who supplied most of the rest of the bones used in the photographs.

My special thanks are reserved for my son, Tim Stirland, who worked very hard to produce the drawings.

Index